WORDS
FROM
SILENCE

———————— • ————————

AN INVITATION
TO SPIRITUAL AWAKENING

———————— • ————————

REVISED EDITION

CONSCIOUS LIVING
PUBLICATIONS

Words from Silence.
Revised edition

Library of Congress Control Number: 2015900377

ISBN 978-1-890580-06-3

First paperback printing February 2015

Printed in the United States of America

10 9 8 7 6 5 4 3 2 1

Library of Congress Cataloging-in-Publication data

Jacobson, Leonard 1944-

Words from Silence. An Invitation to Spiritual Awakening.
Leonard Jacobson

WORDS
FROM
SILENCE

———————•———————

INTRODUCTION

In 1981, I experienced the first of a series of mystical awakenings that would profoundly and radically alter the course of my life. This first awakening involved a deep and lasting opening into love and the truth of life. I experienced the deepest levels of Presence and Oneness and Heaven on Earth was revealed to me. During this time I encountered the living Presence of God. To my amazement, I discovered that God was completely without judgment. God was an allowing God who filled my whole Being with an overwhelming sense of unconditional love and acceptance. The God that I am speaking of has nothing to do with religion. I simply experience God as the silent Presence at the very heart of all things present.

The second awakening, which occurred about three years later, was an awakening into Christ consciousness. During this awakening, the truth about Jesus was revealed. In January 1991, I experienced the third awakening which was a full awakening into God consciousness. I was taken on a journey through the mystery of existence. I became the rocks and the trees and the birds and the sky. I journeyed through time from the beginning to the end and from the end to the beginning. It was profoundly mysterious and not an easy journey to undertake as it involved entry into other realms and dimensions of existence. There have been three more awakenings since then.

The fourth involved revelations about the nature of love and what it means to live lovingly in the world.

The fifth awakening occurred in New York during the summer of 1994, and was an integration of all the other awakenings. It was as though everything fell into place and was somehow integrated within me in the simplest possible way.

Sacred geometrical forms were revealed, which provided me with maps of human and God consciousness that would later prove invaluable in my teachings and the formulation of my message.

After the fifth awakening, I was sure it was over and that my journey was complete. I did not expect anything more and then without warning, the sixth awakening occurred in May of 1997. What took place during this awakening was beyond anything I could have anticipated. It was a profound opening into the mystery of our existence. I felt one with everything. It was as if the sky was my hat and the stars were my friends.

Time disappeared and it was quite clear to me that I had awakened into an eternal and transcendent state of consciousness. It took some time for this awakening to settle and for integration to occur within me.

I have written a number of books which I trust will be of assistance to those who are ready to free themselves from a painful and limited past, and who are ready to awaken into the present moment and transform their lives.

The first book is *Words from Silence*. It contains much of the wisdom revealed to me during the first awakening. *Embracing the Present* is the second book. It follows on from the first, and contains detailed guidance for those on a path of awakening.

The primary focus of this book is on how to awaken fully into the present moment and how to remain awake and present in the activities of our daily living. *Bridging Heaven & Earth* is the third in the series. It is a profoundly mystical work and completes the trilogy. It contains much of what was revealed to me during the second and third awakenings, including the truth about Jesus.

In 2007, *Journey into Now* was published. This book is a complete and comprehensive guide to my teaching. It provides answers to questions that must eventually be addressed by those genuinely seeking to awaken.

More recently, I published *In Search of the Light,* a children's picture book, beautifully illustrated by Fiammetta Dogi, who lives in Florence, Italy.

I share these books with you openly and with all my love. I trust that they will find their way into the hands of those who are meant to read them. In this regard, I am totally surrendered to the will of God.

To be present enhances every aspect of life. It empowers us and frees us from the pain and limitations of the past and anxiety about the future. When we are fundamentally present, we live without judgment, fear, and desire.

We live in a state of acceptance. We live as love in the world. The illusion of separation has dissolved and we live with a strong sense of peace and a continuing awareness of the Oneness of all things.

I invite you to read this book with an open heart.

It is time to awaken out of the bondage of the mind. It is time to awaken out of illusion. It is time to embrace the truth that exists within you, but which is only available to you as you become more and more present. Seek only the truth. It will set you free.

AUTHOR'S NOTE

It has been twenty five years since *Words from Silence* was first published and at least 30 years since I wrote it. My teaching has evolved over the years and I felt that it would be appropriate to update the book. This revised edition contains most of the content from the first edition, but I have added some additional passages to enhance the flow of the book. I have also made some changes to the layout of the book and to the cover design.

My words are not directed towards your mind or that part of you that understands. The truth is beyond understanding, and it arises from the silence at the center of your Being. It is equally available to each one of us as we become present. Whether it is through the pages of a book or in one of my workshops, retreats, or seminars, I am always speaking to that awakened dimension of you which knows the truth. This book is intended to encourage, support and inspire you to become more present, and then you will know from your own experience what I am writing about.

The best way to read this book is to read through it once completely, and then from time to time open the pages at random. The words in this book are powerful. They can inspire you towards your own awakening or they can act as a guide for those already on the path.

Some of the words need to be meditated upon. They are like Koans. The meaning is not always obvious. Some of the words might provoke and upset you.

What you get from this book will depend to a large degree on your willingness to be open and allow some of your most cherished beliefs to be challenged.

The world is at a crucial stage. The opportunity exists now for man and woman to evolve in consciousness. It is as if God has extended to each of us an invitation to participate in a great awakening. This book is a part of that invitation.

I am the magician, the sage and the explorer.
I am the judge, the court jester,
and the innocent child.
I am the eagle and the wolf.
I am the light.
Only the innocent child
can see the light.

I can teach you how to look,
but I cannot teach you how to see.
The innocent child has your vision.

When you are in the past, at an unconscious level,
you are in a dream and you believe
that what you are experiencing is real.
Only when you awaken fully
into the present moment will
you experience what is real.

Wake up!
And discover who you are.

Waking up is one thing.
Staying awake is another.

WHEN YOU AWAKEN

When you awaken,
you know that everything that occurs
at the level of mind is illusory in nature
and so you no longer believe in it as the truth of life.
It is sometimes happy and sometimes sad, because it is a
world of duality. You relax and accept the dual nature of the
world of the mind and the world of experience within time.
This will create balance within duality which will
open the doorway to Oneness.

The whole point of your existence
is to open into Presence and Oneness
and then express yourself fully and authentically
as the unique Being that you are.

You cannot become enlightened
at some time in the future.
You can only be enlightened now.

The truth abides within
and is equally available to all.
It arises when we are fully present
and the mind is silent.

Awakening is a journey for champions.
It is not always comfortable.
It is about encountering yourself at every level.
It is about revealing into consciousness
every aspect of yourself that has been
buried in unconsciousness.
As Jesus said,
"All that is hidden shall be revealed."

When we are truly present,
we emerge from our separate worlds
and come into the one world.
It is in Presence and silence that we
truly meet and come together in Oneness.

If you are fully present in this moment then
you are an awakened Being,
at least for this moment

The future is nothing
but a projection of the past.

Without the past,
how can you create the future?

By glamorizing the past,
you are condemned to repeat it.

Looking back is the same
as looking forward.
There is nothing
but the now.

"What do I want?" is your question.
And what you want is always
changing with the flow.
So go with the flow.

THE OLD MAN AND THE RIVER

An old man walked along the banks of a river.
He was lost in thought and was repeating over
and over to himself the same question.
"What do I want?
What do I want?
What do I want?"
For he had forgotten what he wanted!
He was so lost in thought that he was unaware
of the beauty of the stream flowing past him,
nor could he see the butterflies
dancing around his shoulders.
Suddenly he came to a bend in the river,
and he saw two men sitting quietly there.
One was dressed as a sage.
The other was dressed as a magician.
The sage rose and opened his
arms to greet the old man.

The old man and the river

"You seem troubled, old man," said the sage.
"I have been wandering for many years,"
sighed the old man, "and I am weary.
I keep searching for what I want,
but I cannot find the answer."
"Perhaps my friend, the magician,
can assist you!" said the sage.
The old man looked towards the magician,
who sat very still, with his legs crossed
and his eyes closed.
"How can he help me?" asked the old man.
"If you are to find the answer," replied the sage,
"then you must have the right question.
So the magician is listening to the river
for the right question."
"Will he be very long?"
asked the old man impatiently.

THE OLD MAN AND THE RIVER

The sage was concerned.
"Don't be impatient," said the sage.
"Keep yourself occupied while you are waiting.
Pay attention to everything that is around you.
Listen to the sound of the stream
and to the birds singing.
Feel the flow of the river.
Look at the flowers and the rocks
and the trees reaching upwards towards the sky.
Be still and listen to your own heartbeat.
And just wait."
And so the old man waited. And waited.
He paid attention to everything around
him and everything inside him.
Suddenly the magician stirred.
"I have your question," he said.
But the old man did not move.
"I have your question," repeated the magician,
and the old man turned to hear.

THE OLD MAN AND THE RIVER

"The question is ....." said the magician,
pausing dramatically ....."What do I want!"
"But that is the question
I have been asking all along!"
said the old man.
"Ask it again now," said the sage.
"But I already know the answer!"
replied the old man. "I want nothing!"
"You want nothing," repeated the sage,
with an amused look upon his face.
"Yes," said the old man.
"For while I was waiting,
I saw that, already, I have everything!
I just haven't been paying attention."
And so the old man sat by the river
with the sage and the magician. And they waited.
Just in case some one else wandered along,
who had forgotten what he wanted.

Words stop you from hearing.

Words can help to establish a bridge.
But once the bridge is crossed,
let the words go.

It is far wiser to ask for a
question than an answer.
When you think you have all
the answers, it simply means
that you have run out of questions.

Do not seek the answers.
Let the answers find you.

HARMONY

You can conduct yourself into harmony
with the universe in the same way
that a conductor, with his hand,
conducts an orchestra.
Just listen for the harmony.
Walking with a gentle rhythm
can help to clear the way.

Time and space are illusions
of the mind.
Now is the only time.
Here is the only place.

I live in a dimension beyond space. Here.
And a dimension beyond time. Now.

All that has ever happened
and all that will ever happen
is happening now.

Every moment you have a choice.
Will you be present with what is actually here now,
or will you follow your thoughts into the past
and future world of the mind?

If your commitment is to being present,
there will come a time when being present
becomes your natural state.
The present moment becomes your home.
You will have short excursions
into the world of the mind,
but you never go so far into
the mind that you get lost there.

Beyond good and evil,
darkness exists only as the absence of light.

In truth, you can never be anywhere other than here now.
The experience of being somewhere other than here now
is an illusion, which is created when you enter
the past or future world of the mind, and
become identified with the story
that is unfolding there.

One who is awake
dwells in a state of not knowing
and yet knowing is always available.
When knowing arises,
do not take it into the mind
and convert it into knowledge.
Instead, return to not knowing
and the doorway to knowing remains open.

One who is awake
lives predominantly in the present moment.
The present moment is always recognized
as the truth of life, even when entering
into the mind and functioning
within the world of time.

The only way out is in.

It's not them, it's you.
It's not there, it's here.
It's not then, it's now.

What is, is.
What isn't, isn't.
You become so obsessed
with what isn't,
that you miss what is.

Help yourself, love others.
Love yourself, help others.

In truth, you are love, acceptance, compassion
and you live in the realization of Oneness.
You are empowered from within.
You are an eternal Being.
This is the truth of who you
are when you are present.
But who have you become
on this long journey
through time and separation, living in
a world where no one is really present?

To awaken,
you must be willing to accept
that you are not yet fully awake.

Everything that occurs in your life
is an opportunity for awakening.
There are no exceptions!

FREE WILL

The ability to choose
is at the very heart of free will.
But there is a fundamental choice
which will affect every aspect of your life.
Which world do you choose to live in?
The world of the present moment or
the past and future world of your mind?
One choice leads to truth,
the other leads to darkness.

THE GATES OF HEAVEN

A man was searching for that which cannot be found,
when suddenly he arrived at the Gates of Heaven.
"I want to come in," said the man.
"Then you must come back tomorrow!"
said the gatekeeper.
The man returned the following day.
"I want to come in," he said again.
"Then you must come back tomorrow!"
replied the gatekeeper.
And so the man returned every day
for many years and every day it was the same.
"I want to come in," said the man.
"Then you must come back tomorrow!"
replied the gatekeeper.
Finally the man could stand it no more.
"I have been wanting to come in for many years,"
he said, "but now I no longer want to come in!
My wanting has disappeared!"
"Good! Then no need to come back tomorrow!"
said the gatekeeper, as he ushered the man
through the Gates of Heaven.

THE GATES OF HELL

A man was searching for that which cannot be found,
when suddenly he arrived at the Gates of Hell.
He was about to enter when he was stopped
by an old magician.
"You have no weapons," said the magician.
"Take this sword. It will protect you from
the evil forces that lie within."
"I do not believe in evil forces," said the man,
"so I have no need of weapons."
"Only a warrior can enter the Gates of Hell,"
said the magician, slowly drawing the sword
from its scabbard. And as he did so,
a terrible demon appeared before him.
"Behold the power of the sword!"
said the magician, and with one swift blow,
he killed the demon.
"Now will you take the sword?" he asked.
The man shook his head.
"Are you blind?" asked the magician.
"Can you not see that with this sword
the demon was slain?"
"Are you blind?" replied the man.
"Can you not see that with this sword,
the demon was created?"
And he walked past the magician,
through the Gates of Hell, as if they existed
only as an illusion in the minds of men.

I am a mirror.

What you see in me is yourself.

"Who am I?" is the question.

If you really know
how to ask the question,
the question will disappear,
and the answer will be there.

You are the eyes and ears
of existence.

You are the river hearing itself.
You are a tree seeing the color of its leaves.
You are a flower inhaling its own fragrance.

Wake up!
And discover who you are.

THE TRUE MIRROR

If you want to know who you are,
look into the true mirror.
The flower will reflect your beauty.
The sky will reflect your vastness.
The ocean will reflect your depth.
The child will reflect your innocence.
But if you look into the mirror
that is unconscious humanity,
you are looking into the wrong mirror.
Your reflection will be distorted
by their projections.

THE FACE OF GOD

After searching for many lifetimes,
a man finally arrived at the door of God.
He knocked twice and waited.
Several minutes later,
the door was opened by an old butler.
"I have come to see the face of God,"
said the man.
"What is the point?" replied the butler.
"For many lifetimes you have looked
upon the face of God. Many times,
you have gazed directly into God's eyes,
but not once have you recognized God!"
"Please let me see God," pleaded the man.
"This is my last chance."
"Very well," answered the butler,
"but you must promise to accept the face
you see as the face of God."
"I promise!" said the man earnestly.
"Then come with me," said the butler.
The man followed the butler along
a darkened corridor.
They were carrying torches
which gave off a flickering glow.
At last they came to a room
and as they entered,
the man saw a shadowy figure
sitting silently in the darkness.

THE FACE OF GOD

He stepped forward cautiously,
until the light from his torch
fell upon the face of God.
"This cannot be!" said the man.
"It must be a trick!"
For he was gazing upon his own face,
as if he were looking into a mirror.
"Remember your promise," said the butler.
"If this is the face of God,"
cried the man, "then I am God."
And as he spoke the face
before him began to disappear.
"I have disappeared and now I am God,"
said the man to himself.
He turned to tell the butler that he was God,
but as soon as he saw the butler's face,
he saw the face of God.
"The butler is God," he thought to himself.
"I don't understand."
"Don't try to understand," said the butler.
"Just go outside and look upon the face of God.

THE PRESENCE THAT YOU ARE

The Presence that you are radiates
outwards touching every flower, tree
and mountain, and every distant star.
But it also radiates inwards,
caressing every cell in your body.
It also radiates backwards through time,
embracing, comforting and healing
the child you once were.
It even radiates forwards, affecting
and transforming your future.

DESTINY

It is everyone's destiny
to awaken fully into Oneness.
It is everyone's destiny to be
as awake as Buddha or Christ
and exist as love, acceptance,
and compassion upon this earth.
There is no way to avoid your destiny.
It is as inevitable as the oak tree
emerging from the acorn.

Don't be a Buddhist.
Be a Buddha.
Don't be a Christian.
Be a Christ.

You are awake in Christ consciousness
when you are so fully present that you experience
the living Presence of God in all things present.
In Christ consciousness, you experience yourself
as One with God. In God consciousness,
you have disappeared, and only God is.

GOD IS

God is real.
God is here now.
God is this moment revealed.
For the most part, we are lost in
the past and future world of the mind.
To experience the living Presence of God in all
things present, we will have to come to where God is.
We will have to become fully present.
Otherwise we have no choice but to believe
in God or disbelieve in God and neither is true,
for the truth is beyond belief!

THE DIRECT EXPERIENCE OF GOD

As you become more grounded
in the truth and reality of the present moment,
you will enter into the direct experience of God.
It is not an experience that can be described or defined.
It can only be experienced, and when you experience it,
you will know it.

THE BODY OF GOD

Everything in physical form is the body of God.
Bring yourself present with the body of God
and you will begin to experience
the living Presence of God
in all things present.

The present moment
is never involved in thinking.
Whenever you think,
you must be thinking of something
from the past or something in the future.

You spend very little time
in the present moment.
Reality exists only in the present moment.
Therefore you spend very little time in reality.

When you are in the past,
at an unconscious level, you are in a dream
and you believe that what you are experiencing is real.
Only when you awaken fully to the present moment
will you experience what is real.

If you give up the dream,
you also give up the nightmare.

ABUNDANCE

As you transition from the past and future world
of the mind to the awakened world of now,
you will begin to experience yourself
in an entirely new way.
You will be free of the pain and limitations
of the past and free of anxiety about the future.
You will begin to experience the abundance
that is ever present in each moment.

To awaken into Presence simply means
that you have awakened out of the mind.
You have awakened out of the past and future.
You have awakened out of illusion and separation,
and now you are present.
You are in the reality of the here and now.
You are a fully conscious Being.
You are innocent, open, accepting, trusting.
You are grounded in silence.

When you open fully
into the present moment,
you will feel safe. You will feel connected
to everything. At the deeper levels
of Presence, you will experience Oneness.
At the deeper levels of Presence,
Heaven on Earth is revealed.

CHOOSING PRESENCE

The more you choose Presence,
the more grounded you will become
in the truth and reality of the present moment.
The more grounded you are in the truth
and reality of the present moment,
the more you will experience the sacred
and the divine in those ordinary moments.

If you are to know God, you will
have to give up your belief in God.

I am one of God's alarm clocks.
It is time to wake up.

The only way to be with God
is in total silence.

The only gift you have to offer God
is the gift of Presence.
Give generously.

It is essential to realize how simple it is to be present.
The present moment is always here, waiting for you.
It is constantly inviting you to be present
with what is here, rather than
lost in a world of thought.

If your commitment is
to being present, there will come a time
when being present becomes your natural state.
The present moment becomes your home.
You will have short excursions into the world
of the mind, but you never go so far into
the mind that you get lost there.

Every leaf moving on every tree
is waving to you. It is saying,
"Here I am. Will you not be present with me?"
Every flower is calling to you. It is saying,
"Here I am. Look how beautiful
I have made myself.
Don't you know who I am?
I am God in the form of a flower
and I am trying to attract your attention."

The present moment
is the doorway to the Eternal.
If you stand at the doorway long enough,
God will come to greet you.

At the level of Presence,
you are already complete and whole.
You don't have to grow into it or fix yourself up.
You just have to tune into it.
You just have to wake up.

True awakening involves embracing
every aspect of yourself with love and
acceptance, including everything you have been
denying, hiding or trying to fix. To deny these things
is a judgment of them and judgment will keep you
forever imprisoned within separation.

Awakening to the level of Presence
is a continuing process.
Sometimes awakening can be sudden
and profound, but more often it is
a gentle process that occurs over time.

Once you truly understand the nature
of the mind, you will begin to awaken.
The Master cannot remain asleep
when he or she realizes that
the servant has taken over the house.

Lost in Illusion

Everything that occurs within
the world of the mind is of the
remembered past or the imagined future.
None of it is happening now.
If you are identified with any of it,
you will become absorbed into
the world of the mind.
You will become lost in illusion.

The path of awakening
is not about becoming who you are.
Rather it is about unbecoming
who you are not.

To awaken, you have to encounter yourself
at every level. Leave no stone unturned!

AWAKENING

Awakening involves crossing a threshold
from one level of consciousness to another.
There are three levels of consciousness.
The first is the level of mind.
At the level of mind, your experience of life
is always filtered through the past,
and governed by your beliefs.
When you are in the mind, the focus is on the past
and the future, which are constantly projected
onto the present moment.
The reality of the present moment is never truly
experienced, and the illusions projected
by the mind are mistaken for reality.
You spend your whole life trying to solve
problems, overcome limitations or heal wounds
which are a part of your past and do not exist
in the reality of the present moment.
Life at the level of mind is the world of Maya.
It is a world of illusion.
The second level of consciousness
is the level of Presence.

AWAKENING

This level of consciousness opens within you
as you become more fully present.
You are focused in the here and now,
experiencing the truth and reality
of the present moment.
You are free from the bondage of the past.
You have no anxiety about the future.
You are no longer lost in illusion.
Life is lived in freedom and joy.
You have become grounded in silence.
The third level of consciousness is the Eternal level.
It cannot be defined. It can only be experienced.
It opens up at the deeper levels of Presence,
and it opens up through grace.
At this level of consciousness, there is no time.
Everything is in perfect order and harmony.
You are in a state of perfect silence.
You experience God, Eternity, Oneness.
You are at home in the world of now.

FROM MIND TO PRESENCE
FROM PRESENCE TO THE ETERNAL

To awaken from the past and future world
of the mind into the present moment
is your responsibility.
No one can do it for you.
It is not difficult,
provided you know the way.
I can show you the way, but
I cannot walk the path for you.
If you are sincere, honest, authentic
and act with integrity, and if you are
total in your commitment, you will awaken
from the past and future into the present.
It is your birth right. It is your destiny.
And you will be fulfilled completely,
in this lifetime.
But to awaken from the level of Presence
to the Eternal is another matter.

FROM MIND TO PRESENCE
FROM PRESENCE TO THE ETERNAL

The Eternal opens and reveals itself
as you become more deeply present.
When you are awake in the abundance
of the present moment, and you are feeling
the deepest levels of love, generosity
and gratitude for the moment as it is,
then the Eternal dimension will appear.
You cannot desire it.
You cannot hold onto it.
It will appear when you are ready.
It is not up to you.
All you can do is be an invitation.
Be present. Be grateful. Be generous.
Be honest and authentic.
Then you are the invitation.
And the present moment
will respond to you.

The path of awakening

The path of awakening is clear and precise.
Be present with that which is already present.
Complete and release the past
through forgiveness and repentance.
Do not become too involved in the future.
Feel and express your feelings responsibly.
Own every aspect of yourself,
including those negative aspects of yourself
which you would rather hide and deny.
Surrender judgment in your life.
Stop believing in your thoughts and beliefs.
They are not the truth.
Act lovingly in the world.
Live consciously in the world.
Embrace true responsibility.
Be still.
Be silent.
Be present.
Make sure that there is nothing in your life
that is more important to you
than God and the present moment.
Not your mother, not your father.
Not even your wife or your children.
And certainly not your possessions.
To awaken is your destiny
but it helps to know the way.

THE JOURNEY

There is only one journey.
It is the journey of the soul.
Before the journey began,
the soul existed in Oneness.
In the beginning, the soul's journey was
from Oneness into duality and separation.
The ultimate goal of the journey
is to return to Oneness
but the soul has lost its way.
It has become lost in judgment
and separation.
It has become lost in the need
for purification.
It has forgotten its origins.
It has forgotten where home is.
It is lost in a never ending dream
that continues over many lifetimes.
It is time to wake up out of the dream.
It is time for the soul to find the way home.

AWARENESS OF
UNCONSCIOUS BELIEFS

On the path of awakening,
it is necessary to become aware
of your unconscious beliefs.
It is not a difficult task.
Just become watchful.
If you are alert and watchful,
without any judgment,
your day-to-day life will reveal
those unconscious beliefs to you.
Be a watcher of your self.
Be an impartial observer
of who you are at the level of mind,
which is programmed
with your unconscious beliefs.
It helps to have a sense of humor.

Unconscious beliefs

If you have an unconscious belief
that you will be abused or put down,
you will attract into your life those
who will abuse you or be critical of you.
Your mind seeks to be validated in this way.
"See," it will say to itself,
"I knew I was a victim. I was right all along."
If deep down you feel unlovable,
you will attract into your life
those who are incapable of loving you.
And even those who happen along
who are very loving,
will suddenly find themselves
being unloving towards you.
If you have a belief that the
people who love you will leave you,
then sure enough, it will happen.
Over and over again.
So you had better become
aware of your unconscious beliefs.
They are creating your experience of life.
They are based on your past experiences,
and mostly they are formed in your early childhood.
And as long as these beliefs remain unconscious,
there is no way to be released from them.

THE OLD WOMAN AND THE DOG

The other day, I was taking my dog for a walk.
On the way we encountered an old woman
and as we approached her, I could see that
she was consumed with fear that the dog
would attack her. This fear was absolutely
unwarranted. My dog is absurdly good
natured and has never attacked anything.
As the woman drew nearer,
my dog attacked her.
What else could the dog do?
She had to fulfill her role
in the old woman's reality,
even though it was totally
out of character for her.
Let this be a lesson
for all of us!

THERE IS NOTHING
WRONG WITH THINKING

There is nothing wrong with thinking,
as long as you don't believe in your thoughts as true.
There is nothing wrong with your opinions,
as long as you don't believe in them as true.
There is nothing wrong with your beliefs,
as long as you don't believe in them as true.

To the extent that you are
caught in the emotional pain
and traumas of the past,
you cannot remain present.

When you awaken into Presence,
there is no relationship between
you now and you in the past.
This is simply because
the present moment
is free of the past.
You do not have
to fix yourself up.
That is unnecessary.
Just bring yourself present
and those limiting beliefs
from the past do not exist.
It is as though they never existed.

We are not here to do
anything or achieve anything.
If we do something worthwhile or
achieve something, then that's fine
but we are not here for that.
We are just here to wake up.

Everything that has ever happened
in your life is designed to awaken you.
There are no exceptions.

THE PAST IS STILL WITH YOU

All of your past selves are walking behind you
like a shadow, waiting for you to awaken
fully, and waiting for you to return home.
A return to Oneness, love, truth
wisdom, silence and compassion.
The child you once were is still with you.
He or she is waiting to receive the unconditional
love and acceptance which it has always
wanted and which will finally heal it, calm it
and enable it to relax and surrender
into the vastness of your Being.
Into the light of consciousness.
And it is not just the child
who is walking behind you.
All the identities from past
incarnations are still with you.
The seeker. The pirate.
The highwayman. The sage.

THE PAST IS STILL WITH YOU

Each of them applauding every step you take.
And should you in this lifetime,
go further along the path of awakening
than ever before, then all of your
past life identities go with you.
Your learning is their learning.
Your fulfillment is their fulfillment.
Your completion is their completion.
For they have been on the same journey as you.
Your return home is their return home.
And they will surrender lovingly into you.
For you are the true Master.
You have found the way upon their behalf.
They will disappear into you.
The past will disappear into the present.

Repressed emotions filter through
and distort your experience
of the present moment.

Allow repressed feelings to surface
into conscious and responsible expression
and they will be released from you.

Learn to own and accept
all those aspects of yourself which previously
you have been denying, repressing or judging.
This is a gentle process, which becomes possible
only after you have begun to experience
the present moment at a deeper level.

Come into right relationship with your feelings.
Allow all the feelings repressed within you
to surface into conscious and responsible expression,
for healing completion and release.

If a feeling arises in the moment,
it is telling you how to respond to whatever
is occurring. But if that simple and momentary feeling
is flooded by all the feelings repressed within you
from your past, you can no longer respond
in an appropriate way. Instead, you project the past
onto the present and react, rather than respond.
When you are present, and free of repressed feelings
from the past, then your response to feelings arising
in the moment is always appropriate.

We think to escape our feelings.
If you want to stop thinking and return to Presence,
then feel your feelings.

Most of us have emotions repressed
within us from the past, particularly from
our childhood relationship with our parents.
These emotions filter through and affect every
aspect of our lives and our relationships.

Feel the feelings,
be present with them,
allow them expression in a responsible way,
but do not get involved in the story woven
into the feelings.

LIVING AN AWAKENED LIFE

To live a present and awakened life,
simply be responsive to the moment.
It is very simple. If you are hungry, eat.
If you are thirsty, drink.
If you are lonely,
call a friend for tea.
If you are overwhelmed
with too much company,
then get away by yourself.

ANGER

There is nothing wrong with anger.
It is a beautiful emotion,
as valid and rich as joy or laughter.
But you have been taught
to repress your anger.
Your anger has been condemned.
If anger is unexpressed,
it will slowly poison you.
The key is to know how
to express your anger
in a responsible way.
Do not throw it out onto any one.
No one is responsible for your anger.
Simply express your anger.
Beat up a cushion. Go for a run.
Express your anger to a tree.
Dance your anger.
Enjoy it.

Anger

You are angry because you are
not getting what you want.
It is a sign that you are making
others responsible for you.
No one is responsible for you.
No one is to blame.
You alone are responsible
for yourself.
So if you are angry,
take responsibility for it.
Express it.
Own it.
Enjoy it.
Anger unexpressed leads to violence.
Anger accepted and expressed
in a responsible way
leads to laughter.

RESENTMENT

Most of us live with resentment.
Resentment at not having what we want,
or at having to put up with things
that we don't want.
We never express the resentment,
or we don't fully express it.
And unexpressed resentment
will lead to depression
and illness and eventually even death.
If you express it as anger,
then you will come totally alive.
Resentment is unexpressed anger,
so all you have to do is express your anger.
Resentment puts you to sleep.
Anger wakes you up,
as long as you express the anger
in a responsible way.

To the extent that you maintain yourself
in regret, resentment, guilt or blame,
you cannot be present, simply because
these feelings keep you imprisoned within the past.

In becoming present,
our only interest in the past
is to release ourselves from it.

No one can make you angry
unless anger is repressed within you from the past.
No one can hurt you unless hurt is repressed
within you from the past.

DEALING WITH
EMOTIONAL PAIN

The only way to deal
with emotional pain is to feel it.
The more you can feel it in a soft
and gentle way, the easier it is for you.
It can be soft and gentle.
You can feel it without protest
or complaint or blame.
There is no need to fix it
or make the pain go away.
Just feel the pain. Enter into it.
If the pain is there from the past,
it wants to be experienced.
Things from the past were not experienced,
because they were too painful then.
You were too vulnerable then.
And so you repressed the pain.
These things are waiting to be
experienced so that they can be released.
If you are really gentle with yourself,
you might find that the pain is nowhere
near as large and awesome as you had imagined.
It was your refusal to go near it,
that gave it its size and power.
Approach it and it diminishes.
The general approach I take is
that whatever it is, just let yourself feel it.

Dealing with
Emotional Pain

You don't have to do anything about it.
You don't have to get rid of it.
You don't have to embrace it.
You don't have to understand it
or analyze its origins.
Just feel it. And allow it expression.
If it is anger, then yell and scream
and beat up a cushion.
Express anger as a meditation.
This means that you allow the anger
full and authentic expression,
in a responsible way,
but don't get caught up in the story.
It is from the past and has
nothing to do with the present.
If it's sadness, then cry.
Don't even worry about tissues.
Just let the tears flow.
If it's pain or hurt,
just feel it without complaint
or protest or blame or analysis.
Hidden beneath the anger
and the pain and the hurt,
you will reach to a level
of love and joy within you,
which you have not yet even imagined.

ENLIGHTENMENT

You are in darkness because so much
is repressed at an unconscious level.
Feelings like jealousy, greed, blame, guilt, anger,
fear, resentment, insecurity and unworthiness
are often experienced unconsciously.
You don't want to accept that these things
exist within you, so you bury them
but that does not mean that they disappear.
They simply operate at an unconscious level
so that you might be miserable and in a state of
inner conflict, but you don't know why.
To the extent that these feelings
are repressed, then you are in darkness.
As you allow these things to surface
into conscious awareness then
you are bringing light
to that area of darkness.

Enlightenment

As you allow more and more to surface,
in a spirit of unconditional love and acceptance
without making anyone else
responsible for whatever is there,
then gradually the darkness will disappear.
Until one day you will be enlightened.
It just means that there is no darkness left.
Enlightenment is an ongoing process of allowing
everything up from the darkness of the
unconscious mind into the light of consciousness.
Until one day, the darkness has disappeared.
You are fundamentally grounded in Presence,
and you are a master of your mind and ego.
The illusion of separation has dissolved and you
recognize the Oneness in all things present.

That which you seek is already here.
That which you fear is long gone.

The journey is from here to here.
And the only time you can arrive
is now.

When you are fully present,
you are love, acceptance and compassion.
You are empowered from within and you
live in the realization of Oneness.
This is the truth of who you are.
But who have you become on this long
journey through time and separation?
If you own, acknowledge and confess
who you have become,
it will reveal the truth
of who you really are.

If you are to awaken and
remain fundamentally present, you will
have to free yourself from the past and future.
You will have to free yourself from your story.
Everything outside of this moment is your story.

You can redeem yourself through
prayer, right understanding
and grace.

To redeem yourself is to awaken
from mind to Presence,
from separation to Oneness
and from illusion to truth.

Forgiveness is a powerful force,
which can release the past from you
and you from the past.
Forgive all those who have hurt you
and seek the forgiveness of everyone
you have hurt.
As you are released from the past,
you are more available to the present.

If you are truly repentant for any hurt
you have caused to others because
of your unconsciousness,
you will be forgiven.

Repentance is not true repentance
if there is any sense of spiritual reward.

ACHIEVEMENT

My greatest achievement is silence.
When I sit I just sit.
There's absolutely nothing going on.
I am in silence.
But who will notice?
Who will care?
Who will have eyes to see?
Or ears to hear?
No-one.
And in my silence it will not matter,
for I am not seeking recognition
or acceptance.
I am not seeking anything.
I just am.

ALONENESS

When you can accept
that you are completely alone,
suddenly you will look around
and see that you are not alone.
Existence is all around you
celebrating and you are a part of it.
Life is a dance
and you are the dancer.

It is essential to realize
how simple it is to be present.
The present moment is always here,
waiting for you.
It is constantly inviting you
to be present with what is here,
rather than lost in a world of thought.

When you are present,
you are transcendent
of the mind and ego
and so you can be a witness
to your mind and ego.
You can be conscious of your thoughts
without being lost in them
when they arise.

Awakening is a journey

Awakening is a journey from mind to Being,
from the past and future to the present,
from darkness to light.
It involves awakening to a
deeper level of consciousness.
To a higher level of consciousness.
To an expanded state of Presence.
A state of unconditional
love and acceptance.
A state of silence.

HELPING

To help some one is to violate them.
It implies that they need your help.
It implies that they are helpless.
It is a subtle game of the ego
which puts you up here
and them down there.
I never get the sense
I'm helping anyone.
I'm not helping anyone.
I'm just here.
What you take is what you take.
What you want is what you want.
If it helps you then you're helped,
but I'm not helping you.

Christ is a state of consciousness,
not an individual.
Jesus was an individual
who had awakened to that state
of consciousness.

Only those who reach
to a state of complete inner silence can
know the real meaning of the words of Jesus.
For he was speaking about something
that cannot be known with the mind.
You have to awaken to that level
of consciousness that he was speaking from
if you are to know the true meaning of his words.

God consciousness is the final
stage of the journey.
Christ consciousness indicates that
you are almost there.

THE CROSS AS A SYMBOL

The cross is a symbol representing
the transcendence of duality.
It existed as a symbol of consciousness
long before Jesus was nailed onto it.
Duality can only be transcended
in the present moment.
The present moment is transcendent
of the past and future.
It is the doorway to Oneness and the Eternal.
If Christians are to awaken into the truth of life,
they will have to let go of the past.
They will have to awaken into the present moment.
They will have to let go of the historical Jesus
and find Christ consciousness within themselves.
They will have to take Jesus down from the cross.
They will have to take responsibility
for everything that they are creating in their lives.
If Jesus is taken down from the cross,
then every Christian will have to take his place.

THE CROSS AS A SYMBOL

Every Christian will have to become
his or her own Savior.
You won't have to be nailed onto a cross.
You won't die physically.
It is just the surrender of your ego.
It is the surrender of belief.
It is the end of judgment and separation.
It is the end of life as you have known it.
But crucifixion leads to resurrection.
It leads to Oneness with God.
It leads to truth.
It leads to the Eternal dimension of life.
If you are to be a true Christian,
then you must become a Christ.
You must find your own way
into Oneness with God
just as Jesus found his way
into Oneness with God.
It is time for Jesus to rest.

To believe in God
is an obstacle to knowing God.

One who believes in God can see God
in the symbol of a wooden cross.
One who knows God sees God
in the wood and not the cross.

Awaken from the past and future into the present
and you become a vehicle for God.
You are actively bringing
Heaven to Earth.

ONLY ONE VINE

Judaism, Christianity and Islam are not separate.
They are one vine planted by God.
The ultimate flowering of the vine
will see man ascend to God.
And God descend to man.
A meeting point in the middle.
That meeting point is in Presence.
It is a transcendence of duality.
When the inner is as the outer,
and the above is as the below.
Beyond the light and the dark,
beyond form and the formless,
it is where man and God
meet and become One.

THE FATHER, THE SON
& THE HOLY GHOST

To awaken means that you are
no longer identified with the world
of experience within time.
It means the end of identification
with your thoughts and beliefs.
You are no longer defined by the past.
You are no longer lost in the future.
You know yourself as the one
who exists here now.
You remember the past, you imagine the future,
but you are no longer identified with either.
You have awakened into the present moment.
You have awakened into the truth of life.
You have come to recognize
the eternal nature
of your existence.
At the level of mind, you are the Son.
At the level of Presence, you are the Father.
And beyond you, there is God.
The One.
The Eternal.
The Unknowable.
The Mystery.
The Holy Ghost.

If you want to save the world,
there is only one way to do it.
Save yourself.
To be a Savior for others is to take away
from them their responsibility for themselves.
Everyone has to be their own Savior.
You save yourself by accepting responsibility
for yourself at every level.

To awaken is to become a Christ.
But that does not mean that
you will be like Jesus.
Jesus was Jesus.
You will just be yourself.
You may work in the garden
or the office.
You don't have to become a Savior.
But you will be a Christ.

You get lost because you think
there is somewhere to go.
If you give up believing
in a goal or a destination,
then you cannot get lost.
In the present moment,
there is no destination.

Everything is unfolding as it
should, according to the will of God.
If it happened, then it was the will of God.
If it is happening, then it is the will of God.
And if it will happen, then that is the will of God.

The one who sets off on
the journey of awakening
will not survive the journey.
Such is the radical nature
of awakening.

When you awaken,
you bring consciousness into existence,
and the whole of existence celebrates.
When you awaken, you become a mirror
for existence.

YOU CANNOT PRACTICE
THE TRUTH OF PRESENCE

When I say that you are love,
acceptance and compassion,
that is only true when you are present.
The moment you leave Presence,
and you are caught again in the mind,
you have disconnected from the truth.
You have disconnected from love.
You have disconnected from God.
You are caught in a world
of memory, imagination and belief.
The ego remembers the blissful experience
of love and truth that arises out of Presence.
It then thinks it knows but it doesn't.
It is only a memory of something you experienced
in the past, when you were present.

YOU CANNOT PRACTICE
THE TRUTH OF PRESENCE

The ego never directly experiences anything,
but it remembers the experience
and it then tries to practice it.
This is where religions have gone astray.
They have taken the experience of one who
is awake and given it to the ego to practice.
All of the major religions are based on
the inspirational experiences of the
founders of those religions.
Unless religions have methodologies
to awaken disciples to exactly the same
level of a Christ or a Buddha, then those
religions have failed completely.
They exist only at the level of mind
and have no power to transform us.

Awakening

Spiritual masters have for centuries
been speaking of the need to awaken.
They have said that we are not really awake
and that what we call reality
is in fact a kind of dream.
We live in the world of Maya, or illusion.
What does it mean to awaken?
How can it be said that we are asleep,
even though we are walking around
with our eyes open?
What do they mean by the dream, or Maya?
The answer is very simple.
In order to understand the waking state
you must first look to the sleeping state.
There are three levels of sleep.
The first is when you begin to go to sleep.
It is very shallow. It is a transitional stage
from being awake to falling asleep.
The second stage is the dreaming stage of
sleep. It is during this stage that you dream.
Your eyes move rapidly beneath your eyelids,
which indicates that you are dreaming.
The third stage is deep sleep, which is
a deep and silent sleep, without dreams.

AWAKENING

Your eyes are still. It is during this
stage that you are deeply refreshed.
Whilst there are clearly three stages
of sleep, it is generally considered that
there are only two stages of the waking state.
Waking, and awake.
However, there is in fact a third stage
of awakening, which we rarely experience,
and it is this third stage to which
the Masters are referring.
The first stage of the waking state
is transitional. This corresponds
to the first stage of sleep.
You are no longer asleep, but you are not yet awake.
The second stage, which we generally regard
as awake, is in fact not fully awake and
corresponds to the second stage of asleep.
It is the dreaming stage.
You are actually dreaming,
in the sense that you are in the mind,
unconsciously in the past.

AWAKENING

What is going on in the mind
does not correspond to reality.
It is not what is actually occurring
in the here and now.
Although your eyes are open,
you are in the mind, unconsciously
projecting the past onto the present and
in so doing you distort your sense of reality.
What you may not be aware of is that
there is a third stage of awakening.
Until you reach to this third level of
awakening, you are not yet fully awake.
During this third stage, you are fully
present and your mind is silent just
as it is in the third stage of sleep.
The only difference is that now you are
fully conscious and awake.
You are present with what is here,
rather than lost in the past
and future world of thought.
You can still think, but now you
are choosing consciously to think
and you no longer get lost in thought.
You don't get lost in the dream.

Awakening

You don't have to be present all the time,
and of course there are many times each day
when it is appropriate to think.
The problem arises when you mistake
the dream for reality and you believe that
you are awake when in fact you are not.
Let me be perfectly clear.
During this third stage of awake
there is no activity of the mind.
Your mind is silent.
The past has dissolved
and you are fully experiencing
the reality of the here and now,
free of your projections.
Any thought or reflection concerning
the experience of that reality,
however profound and wise,
belongs to the second stage of awakening
and not the third.
Any thinking, whether conscious or
unconscious, belongs to the second stage
and is part of the dream.

A ROSE IS A ROSE

A man was walking along the street one day,
when suddenly he saw his own ego
walking towards him.
"I know who you are," said the man,
"and I know what you want."
"Do tell," replied the ego.
"You're an illusion," continued the man,
"and you want to exist in illusion."
"Is that so!" said the ego, matter-of-factly.
"You came into being to protect me,
and you've done well," said the man.
"It wasn't your fault I fell asleep.
But I'm awake now. And I'm watching you.
Always! You can't escape my gaze.
The game is up, my friend."
"Do go on," said the ego.
"I am not you. You just think I'm you"
said the man.

A ROSE IS A ROSE

"You exist only in thinking,
and all thinking is an illusion."
The ego was silent for a moment
before replying.
"I am you," he said.
"You just think I'm not."
Just then a sage walked by.
"You are neither this nor that,"
said the sage, pausing for a moment.
"Then who am I?" asked the man.
"A rose is a rose!" replied the sage,
with a laugh.
"Who are you?" asked the man.
"I cannot tell you who I am,"
said the sage. "I just am!"
And he continued happily on his way.

A HIGHER LEVEL
OF CONSCIOUSNESS

Normally we function at the level of mind,
which means that all our experiences
are filtered through the mind.
However the mind can never
participate in the present moment.
It can never participate
in the reality of the here and now.
The mind can only function in the past,
or a projection of the past
which we call the future.
It is possible to awaken
to a higher level of consciousness.
It is possible to awaken into Presence,
where we function not in the mind
but in the truth and reality
of the present moment.
It is in those moments of Presence
that we live an awakened life.

A Bird's Eye View
of the Mind

Awakening to the level of Presence
gives you a perspective which was
not available to you before.
It gives you a bird's eye view of yourself.
It enables you to become watchful
of yourself at the level of mind.
This includes your thoughts,
emotions, attitudes and beliefs.
And all your past experiences which
unconsciously define you and limit you.
The beliefs you formed in early childhood
about yourself, others and life are programmed
into your mind, at an unconscious level,
and define you and affect every aspect of your life.
Until you awaken to a higher level of consciousness,
there is no way to be watchful
of yourself at the level of mind.
The more you are watchful in a spirit
of unconditional love and acceptance,
the more you will become awakened.
You cannot be that which you are watching.
In fact you are the watcher.
In moments of transcendence,
both the watcher and the watched disappear
and all that is left is watching,
which is pure consciousness.
And at the deepest level this is who you are.

The more you watch the mind
without judgment,
the less is its hold over you.

Every aspect of yourself has to be accepted.
Even those aspects you have, until now
been judging and condemning.
As you transcend judgment
and as the energy of acceptance
pervades your Being,
a tremendous
relaxation will occur.

The only longing to follow is the
longing to know who you are.
You can long for a woman or a man.
You can long for material possessions and success.
All of these longings will take you further away,
but the longing to know who you are
will take you home.

MEDITATION

The aim of meditation is to bring
the whole play of mind to consciousness.
If you really understand the nature of the mind
and if you see clearly what it is doing,
you open the way to transcend it.
You transcend to the level of Presence.
You awaken into your essential self.
Some meditations will relax you.
Some will help you to watch the mind.
Some will help you to still the mind.
Some will help you reach to deeper
levels of your Being.
At the very center of your Being
you will enter a state of silence
and love and light, which is truly profound.

THE NATURE OF THE MIND

One of the most basic and primary functions
of the mind is collating, identifying and comparing.
Everything you experience will be processed through
the mind and identified, collated, labelled and compared.
Most of this occurs at an unconscious level.
The mind needs to fit what you are currently
experiencing into its field of known experiences.
Most of the time this collating function
is routine and is not particularly disturbing.
But it deadens you to the reality of the present moment.
It gives you the sense that you already know what
is here, so that you do not really have to be here.
You do not really have to see, hear, feel, touch,
taste or smell what is actually here,
because you already know it.
This knowledge deadens you.
It puts you to sleep.
You miss out on experiencing life,
because your knowledge is always of things past
and never of things immediate and present.
However sometimes this collating function
is not routine and can be very disturbing.

The nature of the mind

There are a number of your past experiences
which were threatening, so that when they
were identified and stored in your mind
as memory, they were given a special tag.
"Danger." "Beware."
Those past experiences which have been tagged,
are usually experiences in your early childhood
which caused you to feel hurt or rejected
and were often followed by feelings of anger.
Any of your current experiences, which remind
you of those tagged experiences will trigger off
your alarm systems and place you on special alert.
In a very real sense, you are regressing to the
earlier experience, projecting it onto the current
situation, and then you react as you did then.
What you legitimately found threatening in your
early childhood is clearly no longer a threat
and yet you are still reacting as a child
according to your childhood reality.
As long as it remains unconscious,
you will continue to do so.

EARLY CHILDHOOD PROGRAMMING OF THE MIND

Here is a list of some of the more common
beliefs about yourself, others and life
which may have been programmed
into your mind in early childhood,
and which might still be unconsciously
determining your experience of life.
Which ones belong to you?
I'm not wanted. I'm not loved.
I'm not lovable. I'm not accepted.
I'm not good enough. I can't do it.
I'm all alone. I'm separate. I'm abandoned.
I can't depend on others.
I have to do it on my own.
It's not safe to trust.
I have to be in control.
It's not safe to relax.
Nobody understands me.
Nobody listens to me. I don't count.
I can't express myself.
It's not safe to speak out. I can't say no.
I can't ask for what I want.
I can't have what I want.
I'm a nuisance.

Early childhood programming of the mind

There must be something wrong with me.
I can't cope. I'm not safe. Life isn't safe.
It's my fault, I'm to blame.
It's their fault, they're to blame.
I'm stuck. I'm trapped.
I don't want to be here.
It's not safe to leave. I don't belong.
I don't fit in.
It's not safe to show my feelings.
I have to hide my feelings.
I have to be good.
I have to do the right thing.
I have to be nice. I must not upset others.
I have to hide who I really am.
I'm not worthy.
I can't trust my own judgment.
I can't trust my own feelings.
I have to be brave.
I have to be strong.
Just to name a few.

THE MIND AND REGRESSION

At the level of mind, you exist as a
collection of memories from the past.
The mind is a like a curtain which acts as
a barrier between you and the reality
of the present moment.
When you are in the mind,
you are somewhere in the past.
Generally, you are not too far
into the past, and so you can function
reasonably well at the level of mind.
But this is not always the case.
Sometimes you experience periods
of stress, worry and anxiety.
Sometimes, you feel upset, hurt or angry.
Sometimes you feel rejected or judged.
Sometimes you feel needy or afraid.
What is happening in each of these
situations is that you are moving further
away from the present moment.

THE MIND AND REGRESSION

You are moving further away from reality.
You have regressed, and it usually
occurs at an unconscious level.
You have regressed to a past experience,
probably from your early childhood
and you are projecting that past
experience onto the present moment.
In a very real sense, you are dreaming
and you are in difficulty because you
believe that the dream is real.
If you could see that you are
simply regressed to a past experience
which you are projecting
onto the present moment,
then there would be no problem.
You would know that what you are
experiencing has no foundation in reality.
You would wake up out of the dream.
Once you can identify the nature
of the dream, it is easy to awaken.

WHEN YOU ARE IN THE MIND

When you are in the mind,
you are so concerned and preoccupied
with the past that you are not really here.
You don't see what is before you.
You simply project the past
onto the present moment.
You super-impose your memory
of some past experience over what
is actually happening now
and you believe that it's real.
Your experience at the
level of mind is illusory.
When you are in the mind,
your experience of life is determined
by all your memories of the past,
and all the limiting beliefs
and repressed emotions
that originate in your childhood.
As you become more and more present,
and as you bring conscious awareness
to everything arising within the mind,
those past memories and limiting beliefs
will gradually dissolve.

THE FEAR OF REJECTION

Because you won't let yourself experience rejection,
the fear of rejection gets bigger and bigger in your
mind and then you seek to avoid it even more.
However, if you allow yourself to experience rejection,
the fear of it gradually diminishes until only a flicker is left.
The fear remains as a flicker, but if you are rejected,
then that is all you will feel, just a flicker of rejection.
And I can assure you that is not a problem for you.
The problem arises when you do
everything to avoid rejection.
In the process, you somehow
deaden yourself to life.

FEAR OF FAILURE

So much of life involves risk
and the possibility of failure.
If you are not afraid of failure,
you will take many more risks in your life.
The more risks you take, the more alive you will feel.
You are afraid of failure because you fear rejection.
The moment you give up seeking acceptance from others,
your fear of rejection will disappear,
and so too will the fear of failure.

FEAR OF
THE UNKNOWN

Whenever you have
had enough of a situation,
whether it is a relationship or work
and you want to leave, the fear of the unknown
will enter immediately to prevent you from leaving.
You will become stuck, caught between the
desire to leave and the fear of leaving.
And you will become increasingly
frustrated, anxious and resentful
until it is resolved.

CONSCIOUS
CHOICES

If you want to awaken,
you might want to consider
the following questions.
"Are the choices I am making
in my life supporting me in Presence
and leading me deeper into peace, love and
Oneness or are the choices I am making leading
me away from Presence and into separation?
Am I acting from fear, or am I acting from love?

LETTING GO OF THE PAST

You don't realize that if you stop looking
backwards craving the love and acceptance
which you didn't receive from your parents,
then you might open your eyes to
what is available for you now.
But you won't let go.
If only you could see that looking back
into an incomplete and imperfect past,
with regret, blame, guilt or resentment
is keeping you from the treasures
that await you here now.
The past has gone.
You cannot rectify something
that is no longer with you.
Just be present with what is here now.
Be grateful for what is here now.

Whenever you are lost in the mind,
don't try to sort it out.
Don't try to fix yourself up.
Just ask yourself,
"How do I return to Presence?"

At the level of mind you exist
only as a memory of your Self.

When you are caught up in
something at the level of mind,
the way back to Presence is simple.
First clearly identify what it is
that you are caught in.
Is it jealousy, fear, unworthiness
or something else?
Identify it. Feel it. Own it.
Express it. Confess it.
Bring it all to consciousness.
Then return to the present moment.

Conditioning
of the Mind

At the level of mind,
you have been conditioned
into beliefs which simply are not true,
and you allow these beliefs to define you.
You are defined according to your sex,
race, religion, and nationality.
All of these things define who you are
and you accept the definition
and live within the boundaries
and limits of this definition.
It is all illusory in nature
and yet you will defend it to the very end.
A Christian will have a totally different
experience visiting Mecca than a Muslim.
But Mecca remains the same no matter who is visiting.
The difference lies solely in the conditioning.
If an Australian and an American listen
to "The Star Spangled Banner,"
their experience of the song
will be entirely different.

CONDITIONING
OF THE MIND

But the song remains the same.
It is this aspect of the mind that leads to
religious and racial prejudice, nationalism,
fundamentalism, and eventually to war.
The cold harsh reality is that you have
been conditioned into believing that these
things really define who you are.
And they do not!
This conditioning imprisons you into
the very outer shell of your personality.
Until you renounce this conditioning,
you cannot break free and move towards
the center of your Being.
Until you let go of this conditioning,
you cannot wake up out of the dream.
You cannot awaken.

KEYS TO AWAKENING

The most important key to awakening
is to learn the art of being present.
It is only from Presence that you
can be unconditionally loving
and accepting of yourself.
This includes all those things
you would like to change about yourself.
Jealousy, possessiveness, control, judgment,
helplessness, inadequacy, blame, guilt, uncertainty,
unworthiness, arrogance, expectation, resentment,
anger, sadness, frustration, just to name a few.
To want to change any of these qualities
in you is a subtle rejection of them,
which is not unconditional acceptance.
The key is to identify, own, acknowledge
and confess all of these qualities,
as they arise within you.
Hide absolutely nothing from yourself.
Own and acknowledge all of these things
with love, acceptance and compassion.
The more you own and accept
whatever arises without judgment,
the more you will relax and be released
out of the past into deeper and
deeper levels of Presence.

Keys to awakening

The second key to awakening is to
come into right relationship with your feelings.
This is only possible as you become present.
There are many emotions from the past
which you repressed, for good reason then.
But now they want to be released,
so it is necessary to find an opportunity
to feel and express repressed emotions
like anger, hurt, pain and sadness.
Just be present with the feelings
whenever they arise within you.
Allow them authentic expression,
but do not identify with the story
woven into the feelings.
The feelings are from the past,
which you are projecting onto the present.
Do not try to get rid of these feelings.
That would be a judgment of them.
Simply allow them to complete
their journey through you.
Once released, they will be gone forever.
It is important to take full responsibility
for your emotional reactions.
No one can make you angry unless you
have anger repressed within you from your past.
No one can hurt you unless you
have hurt repressed within you from your past.

KEYS TO AWAKENING

As these repressed emotions are liberated
from you, you will begin to feel a level of love,
peace and freedom that you did not know was possible.

The third key to awakening is confession. This
has nothing to do with the Catholic idea of confession.
You have not committed any sin which needs to be
confessed in order for you to be absolved.
If you confess these qualities to someone
who is absolutely non-judgmental, and who is
fully present with you, it will help you to own
the quality to which you are confessing.
In your confession, you are saying
"This is me. This is who I have become.
I am possessive and controlling."
Or "I am blaming." Or "I always get angry
when I don't get my own way.
Or "I will not allow myself to get too close
to people because I am afraid I might be rejected."
By confessing and owning it with love,
acceptance and compassion, it is released.
And you are freed to the level of Presence
where none of these qualities exist.
They cannot exist because they are not
a part of the true nature of Being.
They exist only at the level of mind.
If you cannot find someone who is present enough
to receive your confession, then confess to a tree
or a flower, or to God who exists
at the very center of your Being.

Keys to awakening

The fourth key is to come into right relationship
with the ego. The ego is not the enemy.
It is your friend and protector in a painful
world where no one is truly present.
Once you know the ego's true role
in your life, you will come to appreciate it.
You will befriend it, and gradually the ego will
relax and it will allow you to be more present.
As you become established in Presence, the ego will
surrender and its role in your life will be transformed.

The fifth key is to bring conscious awareness
to all the ways that you lose yourself in others.
If you look to others for love, acceptance
or approval, you are losing yourself in them.
If you fear judgment or rejection from others,
then you are losing yourself and you are giving
away your power and your freedom.
To awaken is to come back to yourself,
and release yourself from entanglement in others.

The fifth key to awakening is to accept
full responsibility for yourself.
This will release you from the world of
expectation, resentment, blame and guilt.
It will lead you into total freedom.

The sixth key to awakening is to let go.
Dance. Celebrate. Lose control!

RESPONSIBILITY

To be responsible has nothing to do with others.
And yet it is deeply engraved into your mind
that you are responsible for others,
and that others are responsible for you.
It is the major factor operating in your relationships.
You are responsible for others.
You have to fulfill their expectations.
You are guilty if you fail.
You are to blame.
It's your fault.
You suffer from guilt, blame, resentment and
the heavy burden of responsibility as a direct
result of accepting responsibility for others.
All you have to do is declare yourself
not responsible for others
and these feelings will dissolve.
Then why will you not do it?
Because you cannot declare yourself
free of responsibility for others
without declaring others
free of responsibility for you.
You would have to surrender your expectations
of others completely, which means that no one
is to blame when you don't get your way.

RESPONSIBILITY

No one is to blame when
you don't get what you want,
which throws you back onto yourself.
Responsibility exists in knowing that
every action, every choice, and every decision
you make leads inevitably
to the consequences which follow.
Take responsibility for your choices and decisions
and see that you are creating everything
that is happening in your life now,
whether it is positive or negative.
Once you truly understand and accept this,
you will have entered into true responsibility.
You will have put an end to blame, guilt, control,
expectation and resentment in your life.
If no one is responsible for you,
and you are not responsible for them,
it will change the nature of your
relationship with others.
Your relationships will be based in love
and Presence rather than need or obligation.

THE TRUE MEANING
OF RESPONSIBILITY

There are four aspects to responsibility.
When all four are present in your life, you
can truly say that you are being responsible.
First, you must be able to respond
to whatever is arising in the moment.
There is a difference between
responding and reacting.
A response arises in the moment.
You are present and responding to
whatever is occurring in the moment.
A reaction is based in the past, not the present.
When you react, you are no longer present.
You are re-enacting or re-living something
from the past, which you are unconsciously
projecting onto the present.
When you are present, you will be responsive.
It is your true nature but it has been
conditioned out of you.
If you are hungry, eat. If you are thirsty, drink.
If you are lonely, call a friend.
It is remarkably simple.
Take a dog for a walk.
A dog will teach you about responsiveness.

THE TRUE MEANING
OF RESPONSIBILITY

The second thing is to take
full responsibility for your reactions.
You are constantly reacting emotionally
to people and events in your life.
You feel hurt or angry or misunderstood.
You feel unloved or sad.
And it is always someone else's fault.
Someone else is to blame.
They are somehow responsible for your reactions.
You do not realize that your reactions are
almost entirely due to your conditioning
and your past experiences.
Your experiences as a child unconsciously
determine and define your
experience of others and life now.
You project the past onto the present moment.
Nobody is responsible for your emotional reactions.
Nobody is to blame.
But, of course, if that is true, then you are released
from responsibility for the reactions of others.

THE TRUE MEANING
OF RESPONSIBILITY

The third aspect is to take responsibility
for getting what you want, which means that
you will have to know what you want.
Knowing what you want is
usually a response to a feeling.
For example, I feel hungry.
I want a drink.
Very few people really know what they
want because they are not present.
It is not what they want now,
but rather what they desire in the future.
Wanting is immediate and real, arising
out of the moment, and not the mind.
If what you want arises out of the mind,
then it is a desire aimed at fulfilling
something missing from the past, which
you imagine will fulfill you in the future.
Once you know what you want,
then it is your responsibility to get it.
If it involves other people, ask for what you want
and be willing to compromise.
If it does not involve others, then just do it.
What is stopping you?

THE TRUE MEANING
OF RESPONSIBILITY

Ordinarily we live with expectations
which we don't express, and when
those expectations are not met,
we become resentful, which we hide
until it festers into anger and then hatred.
Expectation places responsibility onto others.
Nobody is here to fulfill your expectations.
Nor are you here to fulfill the expectations of others.
The final thing is that you are responsible
for your own awakening.
This means that you are responsible for whether
you are present or whether you allow yourself
to be absorbed into the past
and future world of the mind.
To awaken is your ultimate responsibility.
And once you awaken, it becomes
your responsibility to remain awake,
which involves remembering to be here now,
and not lost in the mind.
It is a responsibility that has
to be remembered moment to moment.

Feelings of resentment, blame and guilt
are an indication that you are not taking
responsibility for your life or for yourself.

It is easier to blame someone
than to take responsibility for yourself.

Blame is one of the fundamental ways
that we avoid responsibility for ourselves.
Blame keeps you imprisoned in the past.
As long as you continue to blame,
you cannot be present.

There is no one here to save you.
You are your own Savior.
You save yourself by accepting
responsibility for yourself at every level

To give up being responsible for others,
and assume responsibility for yourself
is to enter into your aloneness.
And you will not enter your aloneness.

Freedom and responsibility go together.
You can't have freedom without responsibility.
They go absolutely hand in hand.

Two secret keys

There are two secret keys
to having what you want
and doing as you want.
The first key is to allow others
to have what they want.
And to do as they want.
The more you allow others that freedom,
the more you will have it for yourself.
The second secret key is to be
completely unattached to the outcome.
This gives you absolute freedom
to ask for what you want,
and to go for what you want,
because it will not matter
if you do not get it.

POWER

At the level of mind we feel powerless
and we seek to avoid feeling powerless
by gaining power. But the power we gain
is always in relationship to others.
We feel more powerful than some others, but
there is always the chance that there will be
others who are more powerful than us, and so
our new-found power is indeed precarious.
Power gained in relationship to others
is not power at all.
It is an illusion of power, because it temporarily
relieves us from our sense of powerlessness.
It is false power.
However, it is possible to discover
true power within you.
It arises from the center of your Being
and it is your very life force.
It has no relationship to others
or the world around you.
You are not seeking power over others
and others have no power over you.
It is the power of God.
It is the power of the One.
The more deeply present you are,
the more you will connect
with the source of this power.

LETTING GO OF THE OTHER
ACCEPTING ALONENESS

At the level of mind,
you are always involved with the other.
You either love the other or hate the other.
You want something from the other.
You have expectations of the other.
You try to control or manipulate the other.
You judge the other or you reject the other.
You resent or blame the other
or you feel guilty towards the other.
In any event you are deeply
involved with the other.
Sometimes it is pleasant.
Sometimes it's a nightmare.
But one thing is for sure.
You are not alone.
In order to move from the level
of mind to the center of your Being,
you will have to free yourself
from entanglement in the other.
You will have to gradually surrender your
expectations, resentment, blame and guilt
in relation to the other. But as you let go of
your involvement in the other and before you
connect with the essential nature of your Being,
you are in a kind of limbo.

LETTING GO OF THE OTHER
ACCEPTING ALONENESS

You are no longer connected with the other,
but you are not yet sufficiently connected with yourself,
and so a sense of loneliness arises, a sense of alienation.
Most of you are unwilling to endure this loneliness.
You turn around and resume your connection
with the other, no matter how dysfunctional
that connection might be.
You return to the love, the hate, the
blame, the guilt and the resentment.
It is less painful than being alone.
At least it is familiar.
If only you were willing to
continue on your journey towards the Self.
Eventually you would reach close enough to the
center of your Being that the feeling of
loneliness would disappear and be replaced by a sense
of Oneness, which is incredibly full and enriching.
The more present you are, the more the illusion
of separation will dissolve and the more you will
open into the experience of Oneness.

I'm alone in this moment
but I'm not physically alone.
I'm alone because I don't
have my past with me.
I don't have thoughts or emotions.
I'm just here in my silence,
in this moment, and I am alone.

Don't confuse aloneness
with loneliness.

As you move towards your aloneness,
love at the level of Presence will arise.
Rejoice in it.

NEEDING LOVE

We are deeply conditioned into
a dependency upon each other.
Most songs, novels, poems and movies
glorify this love based on need.
It is all about finding each other
and falling in love.
This wanting and needing each other
is being constantly reinforced
and conditioned into us.
It is continually presented as
acceptable and desirable behavior.
At the end of the movie, the couple's
love triumphs, and they walk off happily
into the sunset.
But they don't show you the sequel
where the couple have grown tired
and fat, are bored and miserable,
and are dependent upon
and resentful towards each other.
Nobody tells you that the key
to fulfillment is not finding each other,
but rather finding yourself.
And you can never find yourself
in the other.

SHARING LOVE

Once you have found yourself
and accepted your aloneness,
then the greatest blessing is to share
the love that arises within you.
Each new moment presents
the richest opportunity to be loving.
And you can share love
in the simplest of ways.
Be soft and gentle.
Be caring and kind.
Be loving in an ordinary
way, without any sense
of wanting anything back.
Life offers you
the most precious gift.
The gift of allowing you
to be present and share love.

If silence is the doorway,
then love is the key.

To love yourself
implies two of you.
Who is the lover?
Who is the loved?

In moments of transcendence,
the lover and the loved
disappear.
And all that is left
is love.

When you are present,
you are abundant with love.
You are overflowing with love.
That is the very nature of Presence
and love is the fragrance of your Being.

LOVE AT THE LEVEL OF MIND

At the level of mind,
that which we call love is not love at all.
It is more accurately called need
and we pursue it relentlessly
because it temporarily enables us
to avoid our aloneness.
But we are alone, so that ultimately
love at the level of mind is bound to fail.
And that is a great blessing, because it
opens up the possibility that you will be
thrown into your aloneness.
Only in your aloneness can you discover the
truth of who you are when you are truly present.
And then you will discover an entirely new
experience of love that is not based on need.
It is your very nature.
It is who you are when you are present.
You are abundant with love.
You are overflowing with love.
You are love. And love is all around you.
At the level of mind, when you love someone
you can be giving, but you
always want something back.
It might be attention or adoration,
or a feeling that you belong or that
you are needed, or that you are special.
And if it is not forthcoming,
then suddenly, love disappears.

UNCONDITIONAL LOVE
AND ACCEPTANCE

We all want to be loved
and accepted unconditionally.
It is a deep longing within us,
which was not fulfilled by our parents.
Because it was not fulfilled
we are still craving it.
We are constantly seeking
love and acceptance from others.
But everyone is in the same sorry state.
Everyone is looking outside of
themselves for love and acceptance.
Those from whom you seek unconditional love
and acceptance have never experienced it.
How can they give it to you?
It is impossible to give to another something
which you have never experienced yourself.
When you don't get what you want,
you begin to feel angry and resentful.
As long as you continue
to seek love and acceptance
from others, you will remain unfulfilled.
When you are present, you are love.
You are acceptance. When you are seeking
love and acceptance from others,
it simply means that you are not present.
You have forgotten who you are.

LOVE ARISING FROM PRESENCE

Love arising from Presence has no relationship.
It's not in relationship to anyone or anything.
It simply relates to whatever is before it.
Whether it is a friend, a dog, a flower or a
tree, the love arising from Presence
will simply extend towards it.
It will embrace it.
And if someone
or something else appears,
then that will be included.
And if you turn and suddenly
see the distant mountain,
then that too will be included.

There is no greater power
than the power of love
which arises from Presence.
It overcomes all resistance.

The love that arises
when you are present
is not selective or exclusive.
It extends to whatever
is immediately before it,
and only to that which
is immediately before it.
It has no memory.

At the level of Being,
you are abundant with love.
You are overflowing with love.
That is the very nature
of your Being.

If you love another,
it simply means that you are love.
Don't get lost in the object of your love.

The truth is that you are love.
It matters not who or what you love.

If you are fundamentally awake in Presence,
you live without judgment, fear and desire.
You live as love in the world.

Love is giving.
It asks for nothing in return.
Love is abundant.
It knows nothing of scarcity.

You cannot hold on to love.
You cannot hold on to truth.
Love and truth belong to the present moment.
Surrender the love and truth of this moment
and you will find love and truth,
like two faithful friends,
waiting for you in
the next moment.

When you can feel the same love
for a dog as you can for your own child,
then you have arrived.

LOVE THY NEIGHBOR
AS THYSELF

Love thy neighbor as thyself,
because thy neighbor IS thyself.
Thy neighbor includes
every living human being, regardless
of their religion, race or nationality.
Thy neighbor includes every mountain,
flower and tree, and every bird,
animal and creature of the sea.
There is only One and everything
in physical form is an expression
of the One.

The love that arises from Presence
is like the full moon
on a cloudless night.
It casts its light upon all,
without selection
or discrimination.

God and the present moment respond
most fully to love, gratitude,
generosity and humility.

When you are fully present,
you transcend duality and open into Oneness.
In Presence, there is power without opposition.
There is love without hate, acceptance without judgment
and allowing without control.

RELATIONSHIP

Relationships by their very nature
are based in the past and future.
They exist as a construct within the mind.
We feel more secure in relationship
because we believe that others
will be there for us in the future,
which helps us escape
from the pain of being alone.
It helps us escape the pain of separation
and the pain of living in a world
where no-one is truly present.
But this mechanism of escape
will take you out of Presence
and imprison you within the mind.
Then you will be caught in the past.
You will bring your incomplete
relationships from the past,
particularly with your mother and father,
and project them onto your current relationships.
You will project all your unhealed wounds
and unfulfilled needs into your relationships.
Then your relationships become contaminated
with expectation, resentment, blame, guilt,
judgment and issues of control.

RELATING

Relating can only be in this moment.
No past. No future.
With relating there is no projection
of the past onto the present.
And there is no anxiety about
what might happen in the future.
When you relate to someone, you are present.
You are spontaneous and you have no expectations.
There is no attachment because you are focused
in the moment rather than in the past or future.
This does not mean that you cannot live
with someone and share a life together.
It just means that the focus will be much
more on relating than on relationship.
With relating, there is no ownership.
There are no guarantees of security.
You cannot be sure that the person
with whom you are relating will
be there for you in the future.
But that keeps you alive and vibrant.
It keeps you at the edge of the unknown.
It prevents you from taking
each other for granted.

THE VALUE OF RELATING

In the past, people who were involved
in the pursuit of higher consciousness
all finished up in the mountains or a monastery,
or an ashram because society
would not allow a place for relating
as an alternative to relationship.
It is too disturbing for those in relationship.
But I say to you that it is time for society
to learn the value of relating.
It is no longer enough that our conscious
Beings remove themselves from society.
Higher consciousness has to be integrated
into our everyday lives.

Each new moment

Each new moment presents
an opportunity for conscious choice.
We can choose to let go of the past.
We can choose to be here now.
We can choose to accept
responsibility for ourselves.
We can choose to give up blame, guilt,
expectation and resentment.
We can choose to surrender
our patterns of control.
We can choose to respect and care
for our bodies and our environment.
We can choose to be loving and compassionate
towards each other and towards
all of God's creation,
particularly those awake and present Beings
which we refer to as animals.
We can choose to awaken.
Or we can choose to remain asleep
and unconscious.
Whatever we choose, we will have to live
with the consequences that inevitably
flow from the choices we make.
In that way, we are indeed responsible
for ourselves.

LIVING WITH THE UNKNOWN

In relationship, you gain security
by owning each other.
He is mine. She is mine.
This ownership kills you
and it kills the relationship.
Ownership brings with it control,
restriction and limitation
which deadens you to life.
It is only by allowing yourself to live
in a state of not knowing that you
remain open to life and feel fully alive.
Each new moment
is pregnant with the unknown.
If you can live with the unknown,
then sooner or later, you will enter
into the unknowable.

DEATH AS A PART OF LIFE

Death is an essential part of life.
If you run from death you will miss life.
You must be willing to die constantly, in the sense
that each moment you are dying to the past,
in order to move more fully into the present.
If you do not allow this, you cannot feel fully alive.
If you are afraid of death and dying, you
will not allow yourself to die to the past.
You will be unable to move into the present,
where life and reality exist.
You hold on to the past
because it is known to you.
You are familiar with it.
You feel safer with the known.
But death is never the end.
Death simply signifies
the end of the old and the known.
It also heralds the arrival of the new.
And the new, by its very nature must be unknown.

FEAR OF THE UNKNOWN

You cling to the known and fear the unknown.
This stems from birth which was your very first
experience with the unknown, from
which you have never fully recovered.
From the beginning of your life at the point
of conception, until your birth, your only
experience was inside your mother's womb.
It felt extremely safe.
All your needs were attended to.
Your mother fed you, breathed for you, digested
your food, circulated the blood, and protected you.
She was totally connected to you in every way.
It felt good. Almost like Paradise.
And since it was all you had ever known,
it seemed like Eternity in Paradise.
But you were thrown out of Paradise.
You were born. Into the unknown.
And it was a very traumatic experience for you.
Your experience of separation at birth
was so dramatic that you still feel separate.
If you had been able to relax, you would have
gradually recovered your sense of connection.
And so you would have learned that your first
experience with the unknown, although traumatic,
actually led to a state of expansion.
It led to an increased sense of connection.

FEAR OF THE UNKNOWN

You were simply moving from a womb which
had become too small for you to a larger womb.
The womb of existence.
But you did not complete the move.
You tensed up.
You contracted.
You did not feel safe.
And so you are left with
a fear of the unknown that is unwarranted.
You have to give the unknown another chance.
You will discover that the unknown
always leads to expansion and growth.
To choose the known leads to
contraction and death.

LETTING GO OF THE PAST

The reason that experiences from the past
become stuck and are still with you is that you
did not allow yourself to fully feel the feelings
associated with the experience at the time.
As a child, the feelings were too much for you
to deal with. And so the experience
and the feelings remain repressed within
you at an unconscious level.
These feelings can sometimes
originate in previous lifetimes.
When you allow yourself to experience those
emotions from the past, then that past
experience can be completed and released.
If you were angry at your father
for some reason as a child,
but you repressed that anger,
then that anger is still within you
and will emerge at times inappropriately.
You will project your anger at your father onto
others. But if you express that anger, in the right way,
imagining that your father is in front of you,
then that anger from the past can be released.
You will have to play two roles at once.
On the one hand, you are allowing the anger
to surface and you are expressing it fully.
You are saying everything to your father
that you could not say as a child.

Letting go of the past

You are holding him accountable for hurting you.
On the other hand, you are so fully present
that you are completely unidentified with
the story that the anger is revealing.
You know that it is from the past and it
has nothing to do with the present moment.
It is the same with the feelings of rage, sadness,
helplessness, fear, insecurity and unworthiness.
To cut yourself off from the feelings of an
experience is to hold a part of yourself down,
and that can last a lifetime.
People often feel tremendously alive
and energetic when they allow these feelings
from the past to be experienced and expressed.
It is because all the energy used to suppress
those feelings is suddenly liberated.
You can allow full and total expression of anger,
sadness, rage, helplessness or hopelessness
without becoming identified with it.
Don't take any of it seriously.
It has nothing to do with
the reality of the present moment.
There is nothing to be afraid of.
In fact, fear arises as a result
of avoiding those emotions.
Feel and express the emotions
and fear and anxiety will disappear.

BEYOND
UNDERSTANDING

When you are in the mind,
you want to understand everything.
When you understand, it gives you
the feeling that you are in control.
But the truth is beyond the
mind's capacity to understand.
You cannot understand truth.
You can only know truth.
And that knowing arises from the
silence at the center of your Being.
It arises when you are truly present.
When knowing arises in the moment,
be careful. For the mind will want to claim
it as its own and make itself knowledgeable.
The most that the mind can manage
is a memory of that knowing.
It is your need to understand that takes you
out of Presence and into the mind.
It is your need to understand
that separates you from the source of truth
that is ever present within you.

The primary purpose
of the mind is survival.
Congratulations!
You have survived.
Now what will your mind do?

At the level of mind,
you exist within the world of duality.
Awakening to the level of Presence
involves transcending duality.
If you are to transcend duality,
you will have to bring duality
into balance within you.

The mind will create a thousand problems
so that it can find a thousand solutions.

From the many parts of mind to the unity of Presence

At the level of mind, you are divided
into many conflicting parts.
The part that thinks you are unlovable
and the part that feels unloved.
The part that is self critical
and the part that feels criticized.
The part that judges
and the part that feels judged.
The part that is pushing you
and the part that feels pushed.
The part that rejects certain things
about you and the part that feels rejected.
The part that says go forward
and the part that says go back.
The part that feels bored and wants adventure
and the part that is afraid of the unknown.
The part that is angry and the part
that represses your anger.
The part that wants to be in control
and the part that feels controlled.

FROM THE MANY PARTS OF MIND
TO THE UNITY OF PRESENCE

The part that wants to be alone and
the part that wants to be with others.
The part that is afraid of intimacy
and the part that is afraid to be alone.
Can you see that with all these conflicting parts,
you have little chance of any kind of resolution?
A duality of two parts, mind and Presence,
is a vast improvement over the many
parts of the personality.
Presence accepts mind
and in that acceptance,
mind surrenders into Presence.
In moments of total surrender,
mind disappears,
and only Being remains.
Duality is transcended.
Oneness is revealed.

HEALING THE PAST

The present moment contains within it
the true past and the true future.
You can gain access to the past
through the doorway
of the present moment,
and a profound healing can occur.
With the right guidance, you can change the past.
You can complete the past. You can release the past.
But this is only possible from the deepest
levels of awakened Presence.

THE JOURNEY HOME

As I give up my attachments,
as I give up my involvement in the past,
and as I give up trying to find myself in others,
I return to the silent presence of my Being.
I become flooded with light and love.
And don't think for a moment
that I am special.
This is available to anyone who wants
to undertake the journey home.
To the inner home of your Being.
And you don't have to go all the way.
Just a few steps and your whole
life begins to change.
After the first few steps,
you will know that what I am
saying is true and you will
want to travel further.

LOOKING BACK

If you must look back into the past, then
look back with understanding and compassion.
Your parents were incapable of giving
you unconditional love and acceptance,
which was what you really needed.
It was the first thing you needed
because it was the only thing that
would make you feel safe and secure.
It is the source of all your desire.
And you didn't get it.
We are only capable of sharing
that which we know.
Your parents didn't know anything about
unconditional love and acceptance
because they had never received it
from their parents.
And their parents had never received it.
So you can see that no one is to blame.

LOOKING BACK

It just happened, because of the degree of
unconsciousness at a collective level.
All that can be done now is that you take
responsibility for your own awakening
and the chain of unconsciousness
will be broken, at least for you.
And if enough people begin to awaken,
even just a little, it will begin to impact
at the collective level.
So what are you going to do?
Are you going to keep looking
backwards, full of anger,
resentment and unfulfilled desire?
Or are you going to be here now?
Because everything is available
for you in the here and now.
Love, truth, compassion, silence,
bliss and Oneness.

LIVING IN THE MOMENT

Start living in this moment and for this moment
rather than for those abstract future things
which the mind chooses to live for.
What is real is whatever
is actually here in
the moment with you.
Nature is abundant.
There is more than enough
for you to be present with.

RESPONSIBILITY

When we learn to take responsibility for
ourselves, then we will start taking
responsibility for the planet.
The planet is being destroyed by
our abandonment of responsibility.
We assume that we own the planet.
And ownership confers upon us
the right to do as we like.
We do not own this planet.
We are simply guests here.

THE SEED

You might have
to adjust your life
so that you have more
moments in Presence.
We live almost exclusively
in the domain of the mind.
Sometimes the adjustments have
to be radical, but that is up to you.
Being present will cause the seed of
Presence to flower and it is the full flower
of your Being which contains the real treasures.
Love, light, truth, compassion, bliss, and Oneness.

You need to pull the weeds out from around
the flower if the flower is to fully blossom.

I am not telling you what to do.
I have no judgment about the activities
of the mind. I am not suggesting that
those activities ought to cease.
I am simply saying that
being present will nurture
the seed of Presence.

The seed of Presence
grows in the here and now.
It cannot grow anywhere else.
Just like the seed of the flower will
only grow in soil, the seed of Presence
will only grow in the here and now.
The here and now is soil for the seed of Presence.

THE SEED
AND THE FLOWER

As you awaken,
you will begin to experience
the flower of your Being.
But the full flower of your Being is too vast.
You cannot embrace it for long.
It is necessary to let go of the flower
and embrace the seed.
In time, the seed will evolve into the flower
and eventually the flower will come to full bloom.
And I will tell you something
that very few people know.
Once the flower has come to full
bloom and you have lived and expressed
and experienced that flower totally,
that flower will be replaced by a second flower
which is even greater than the first.

Don't Be in a Hurry

Don't be in a hurry.
Watch a flower grow.
It is not in a hurry.
It does not compare itself
with other flowers.
It does not wish to be
some other color
or some other shape.
The flower does not try to bloom.
As long as the conditions are suitable,
it will come into full bloom
and the flower trusts that.
So just relax and be present with
whatever is here in the moment with you.

THERE IS NOTHING
WRONG WITH THINKING

There is nothing wrong with thinking.
There is nothing wrong with entering the
world of the mind, as long as you know
that you are entering a world of illusion,
and you know that only the present moment
is the truth of life. Then you can play
in the world of time, with your thoughts,
memories, and imaginings.
Enjoy yourself, but be careful!
It is easy to get lost there.

IT IS TIME
TO AWAKEN

It is time for humanity
to awaken at a collective level.
Enlightenment can no longer be for just
a select few who no longer participate in the world.
If there is to be an awakening at a collective level,
we will have to learn to function within the world.
This means that we will have to find a balance
between the timelessness of the fully awakened
state and the world of time.

You can live in a house
but your real home
is inside you.

It is only when you are
fully present that you will
discover that your real home is within.
When you are no longer looking for
a home outside of you, the whole
of existence becomes your home.
Your home knows no boundaries.
You are at home in the universe.

You have a vast family,
an extended family.
The whole of existence
is your family.

TRUST IN EXISTENCE

Once you awaken and as you
continue to awaken to deeper levels,
then seek out and create the environment
appropriate for that level of Presence.
Find what suits you. Make your life
an expression of your authentic self.
Make it a declaration.
Nothing is gained by comparing
yourself with others.
Allow your Being to unfold
and express itself in its own way.
And the difficult thing is that
you don't know exactly what that is.
You have to be in a relationship of deep trust
with existence and allow your life to unfold.
And I can tell you that what was appropriate
for you at the level of mind may no longer
be appropriate at the level of Presence.
I am not saying that it will become inappropriate.
I am simply saying that you can't hold on.
This creates fear and uncertainty for the mind,
but exhilaration and freedom for the Being.

It has been said,
"Be in the world,
but not of the world."
To say that I am not of this world
simply means that I am not
attached to anything.
Nor am I identified
with the story that is unfolding
within the world of time.

If I am not of this world
then I am not attached to anything.
Not to people or things or outcomes.
My wanting brings me into the world.
My not wanting also brings me
into the world.
It is my attachments
that render me of this world.

Only those who are innocent
can experience Heaven on Earth.
This has nothing to do with
the absence of sin or freedom from guilt.
An innocent is one who is willing to be
in a state of not knowing.

Desire takes you into the future.
You can never be fulfilled in the future.
You can only be fulfilled now.

All attachments prevent you
from being present. In the present
moment, you cannot hold onto anything,
nor are you identified with anything.
You are simply here, present
with what is here.

BEYOND BOUNDARIES

In order to have a sense of your individual identity,
you must have a sense of your own boundaries.
Your physical body is one of your boundaries.
Your energy body is another.
It is essential to maintain your boundaries
in a state of good repair if you are to be
an empowered individual
with a strong sense of your essential self.
No one has the right to intrude into you.
No one has the right to penetrate beyond your boundaries.
To do so would be a violation of you and would lead
to confusion within you about your identity.
You would begin to lose touch with your essential self ,
as outside influences and energies enter into you
and contaminate your sense of who you really are.
Only those whose boundaries are clear and intact will
be able to awaken into a state of Presence at such
a deep level that boundaries begin to dissolve.
Only those who maintain and protect
the integrity of their boundaries
will be able to awaken into
the Oneness of all things.
We have to separate from each
other to come to Oneness.
Such is the paradoxical
nature of our existence.

ONLY YOU

The inner dimension of your Being
is meant to be clear and uncluttered.
We intrude into each other in so many ways.
We intrude with our needs and expectations.
We intrude with our thoughts and opinions.
We intrude with our judgments.
We intrude with our blame.
We intrude with our stories.
We intrude with our beliefs.
When you clear these things out of you,
you will open into the deepest level of inner silence.
God wants you whole. God wants you pure.
God wants you fully present.
And God wants you silent.
It is in the silence and the Presence
that you will begin to experience
the living Presence of God
at the very heart of silence
within you.

The heaven you believe in
is the heaven of the mind.
It is an illusion.
Heaven is possible now.
In fact, it is only possible now.

Transcendent of all experience,
I am the one experiencing.

One who knows
lives in a state of not knowing.

In moments of transcendence,
I disappear and only God remains.
But when those moments have
passed, then I am not God,
nor am I the son of God.
I am just me.
But I know
that God is
and that I am
and that God and I are One.
And the whole of existence celebrates.

Whenever someone awakens fully,
it affects human consciousness
at a collective level.
It is like dropping a stone
into a dark murky pond.
Ripples of light!
Not one word
need be spoken.

THE HIGHEST FORM OF PRAYER

The highest form of prayer is be present
and offer yourself to God.
Offer your eyes to God so
that God may see the sunset.
Or a flower.
Or a leaf falling gently to the ground.
For God has no eyes other than your eyes.
Offer your ears to God so that God
may hear the sound of a bird singing.
Or the laughter of a child.
Or a frog jumping into a pond.
For God has no ears other than your ears.
Offer your hands to God so that God may
touch the bark of an ancient tree.
Or feel the coolness of the water in a flowing stream.
For God has no hands other than yours.

Your gift to God is honesty.
God's gift to you is Truth.

Nothing is silent.
Nothing is full of love.
Nothing defines who you really are.
Nothing is beyond contradiction.
Nothing is without beginning
and without end.
Nothing is perfect.

Become full of nothing.

I think.
Therefore I am not.
I think not.
Therefore I am.

VISIT TO A ZEN MASTER

A very learned man travelled a great
distance to visit a Zen Master.
"I have journeyed far," said the man.
"And I have many questions to ask you."
"What is the point?" replied the Zen Master.
"Your mind is so full of knowledge and
attitudes and beliefs that there is no room
for my answers to enter. It is better if you
leave now. Drop your knowledge. Throw out
your opinions and beliefs and meditate.
When your mind is completely empty,
you may return with your questions."
The man left and for the next two years,
he followed the Zen Master's advice.

VISIT TO A ZEN MASTER

He meditated daily.
He dropped all that he knew
and everything he believed in
until at last his mind was empty.
He returned to see the Zen Master.
"I am in a state of no-mind,"
said the man blissfully.
"Now you can ask your questions,"
said the Zen Master.
"But my questions have disappeared,"
said the man. "I have no questions."
"Good," replied the Zen Master.
"For I have no answers."

ABOUT THE AUTHOR

Leonard Jacobson is a modern mystic and spiritual teacher who is deeply committed to guiding and supporting others in their journey towards wholeness.

He was born in Melbourne, Australia in 1944 and was educated at the University of Melbourne, graduating with a law degree in 1969. He practiced law until 1979. He then set off on a long journey of spiritual discovery which took him all over the world, from the United States to the Middle East, India, and Japan.

In 1981, he experienced the first of a series of spontaneous mystical awakenings that profoundly altered his perception of life, truth, and reality. Each of these enlightenment experiences revealed deeper and deeper levels of consciousness, filling his teachings and his writings with wisdom, clarity, love and compassion.

He has been running workshops and seminars for more than thirty-two years, offering inspiration and guidance to those on a path of awakening.

He lives near Santa Cruz, California and offers evening teaching sessions, weekend workshops, and longer residential retreats in the United States, Europe, Japan, China and Australia.

Leonard Jacobson is the founder of The Conscious Living Foundation, a registered non-profit organization. In 2005, he was awarded the Peace Prize by Religious Science International, although he is not affiliated or associated with any religion or church.

His teaching is both inclusive of and transcendent of all religions and spiritual traditions. It is for all those genuinely seeking to awaken, and for all those who do not yet realize that they are genuinely seeking to awaken.

In addition to *Words from Silence*, he is the author of four books. *Embracing the Present, Bridging Heaven on Earth, Journey into Now*, and his latest, *In Search of the Light*, a beautifully illustrated children's picture book.

His books have been published in many countries including South Korea, Japan, Taiwan, China, Holland, Denmark, Poland, Lithuania, and the United States.

You can learn more about Leonard Jacobson
at www.leonardjacobson.com